W9-BIY-271

Child Abuse

Look for these and other books in the Lucent Overview series:

Abortion
Acid Rain
AIDS
Alcoholism
Animal Rights
The Beginning of Writing
Cancer
Child Abuse
Cities
The Collapse of The Soviet Union
Dealing with Death
Death Penalty
Democracy
Drugs and Sports
Drug Trafficking
Eating Disorders
Endangered Species
Energy Alternatives
Espionage
Extraterrestrial Life
Gangs
Garbage
The Greenhouse Effect
Gun Control
Hate Groups
Hazardous Waste
The Holocaust
Homeless Children

Illiteracy
Immigration
Money
Ocean Pollution
Oil Spills
The Olympic Games
Organ Transplants
Ozone
Pesticides
Police Brutality
Population
Prisons
Rainforests
Recycling
The Reunification of Germany
Smoking
Space Exploration
Special Effects in the Movies
Teen Alcoholism
Teen Pregnancy
Teen Suicide
The UFO Challenge
The United Nations
The U.S. Congress
Vanishing Wetlands
Vietnam
World Hunger
Zoos

Child Abuse

by Tom Ito

LUCENT
B·O·O·K·S

LUCENT Overview Series

Library of Congress Cataloging-in-Publication Data

Ito, Tom.
    Child abuse / by Tom Ito.
        p.   cm. — (Lucent overview series)
    Includes bibliographical references (p.   ) and index.
    ISBN 1-56006-115-4 (acid-free paper)
    1. Child abuse—United States—Juvenile literature.   [1. Child
abuse.]   I. Title.   II. Series.
HV6626.52.I76   1995
362.7'6'0973—dc20   94-17274
                                                                            CIP
                                                                             AC

Contents

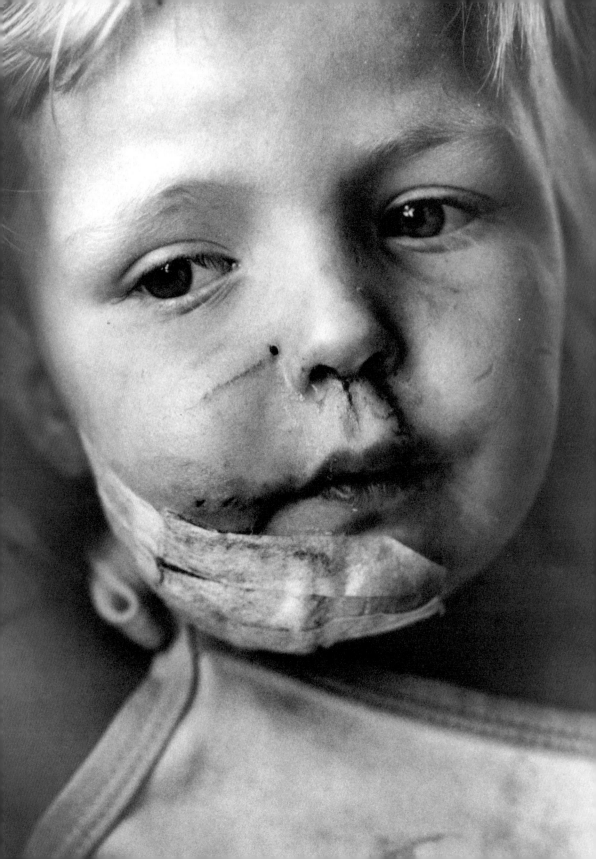

Introduction

CHILDREN ARE OFTEN referred to as being our greatest natural resource. They represent the human potential for intelligent achievement, creative expression, and individual integrity. One of the greatest challenges of society today is the necessity of protecting children from emotional and physical abuse.

Children are the most vulnerable members of society. They are dependent on adults for food, shelter, the emotional nourishment of love and encouragement, and the guidance of healthy discipline. The abused child is denied this support and security. Many have been subjected to the traumas of physical violence and are whipped, beaten, or subjected to other forms of physical mistreatment. Surveys report an alarming increase in the number of children who fall prey to crimes of incest and sexual molestation, as well. In addition, there are reports of a growing number of children who become victims of emotional and psychological mistreatment. They are belittled, threatened, or neglected and deprived of food, shelter, and clothing or the reassurance of parental encouragement and companionship.

Research conducted by such government agencies as the U.S. Advisory Board on Child Abuse

(Opposite page) More than a million children in the United States are abused or neglected each year. As the number of child abuse cases continues to climb, our society grapples with the difficult challenge of protecting children from physical and emotional mistreatment.

and Neglect indicates an alarming increase of child abuse in the nation. A survey conducted by this board in June 1990 estimated that the number of reported child abuse cases has increased by 200 percent since 1977. In 1990 alone, social workers confirmed more than 1.5 million cases of child abuse or neglect in the United States.

The growing number of suspected child abuse incidents reported in the United States has resulted in the development of a number of complex moral and legal dilemmas. Many critical issues have arisen as public concern over child abuse has grown. Some of these issues include establishing clear and accurate guidelines defining abuse and concerns about the protection of family privacy while investigating cases of suspected abuse.

Efforts in society to deal with these and other problems regarding child abuse have been intensified by strong public outrage over the mistreatment of young people. Child abuse is regarded by society as one of the most repulsive

Marchers in Boston express their outrage over the sexual abuse of children. As public awareness of the problem of child abuse increases, so do society's efforts to deal with it.

and horrifying of all crimes. Family violence, incest, or sexual molestation involving children and adolescents by adults often arouses public reactions of anger, disgust, and horror. As a result, child abuse has become an intensely emotional issue in our society.

The American public's awareness has also grown regarding the possible long-range emotional and psychological harm inflicted on child abuse victims. Such victims often suffer from feelings of severe guilt and fear, loss of self-esteem, and other mental or emotional disorders resulting from the trauma of their abuse. According to a report issued by the Department of Health and Human Services in 1992, research has shown that suicide, violence, delinquency, drugs and alcohol abuse, and crime are often related to past child abuse experiences. Knowing this, researchers have set out to find effective ways of preventing this abuse.

The growing number of physicians, psychologists, counselors, educators, legislators, lawyers, clergy, and private citizens concerned with the effective prevention and treatment of child abuse indicates the tremendous scope and complexity of the problem. This increasing involvement has encouraged a public realization that the crisis of child abuse must be addressed with concern and compassion balanced with awareness and understanding.

Child abuse has been described by the U.S. Advisory Board on Child Abuse and Neglect as a national emergency. Many people also consider it to be a national tragedy. Children and adolescents are the most vulnerable citizens of society. The quality of their lives and the protection of their welfare is a responsibility entrusted to adults who possess the power to safeguard the most precious human resource of any nation.

A doctor hugs a patient during her hospital rounds. Physicians and others who work to prevent and treat child abuse are faced with a complex and widespread problem.

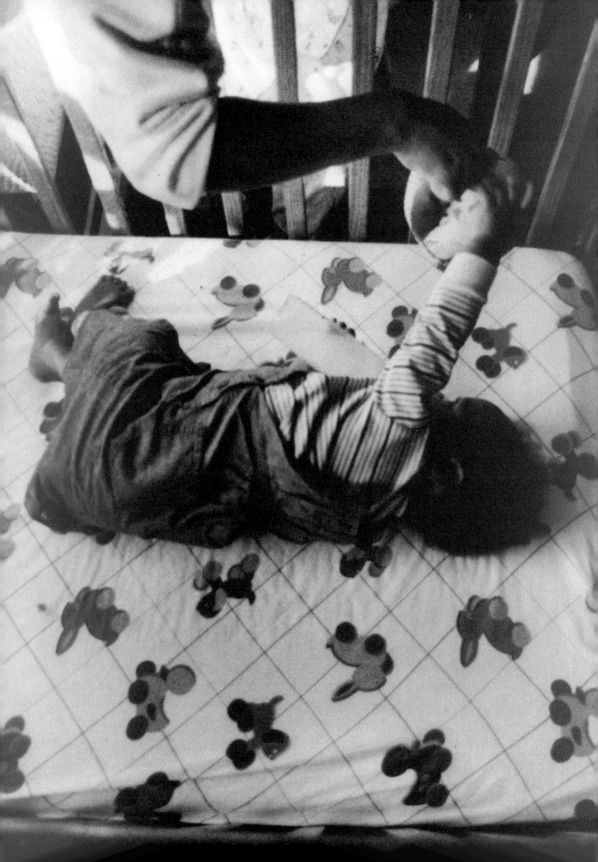

1

A Crisis
of Conflicts

"I AM ALONE, reaching for your love, but I am cut . . . by the pain. . . ." These words were written in a poem composed by a young victim of child abuse. They express the loneliness, fear, and torment suffered by countless children who are physically and sexually abused by adults. The abused child often feels alone and helpless in such harmful relationships, and the trauma of abuse often has devastating effects on victims.

Child abuse today is recognized by the general public as a major problem in the United States. Social service workers and other child care experts investigating such cases report an alarming increase in incidents involving young children and adolescents who have been beaten, burned, tied up, starved, sexually assaulted, and in some cases, killed by parents or other adults.

Reports by caseworkers investigating suspected incidents of child abuse reveal that such mistreatment occurs in many ways: A teenage mother unable to cope with the stress of being a parent becomes enraged and slaps her baby whenever the child begins to cry. A father repeatedly forces his adolescent daughter to engage in sexual acts with him and threatens to kill her

(Opposite page) A shelter worker helps a child from an abusive home feel more secure. Harmed by the adults who are supposed to love and care for them, abused children often feel helpless and alone.

11

unless she remains silent about the abuse. Two children are found tied and gagged in a closet where their parents left them as a punishment for disturbing their sleep. A boy is repeatedly burned by a hot iron by parents who are under the influence of alcohol and cocaine.

The hidden suffering

Many of these crimes occur in the privacy of the victims' homes and are never reported to the authorities. Experts are concerned about the possibility that countless young people suffer and sometimes die from mistreatment because of such secrecy. In addition, many therapists believe that such unreported cases prevent abusive adults from receiving needed counseling and treatment. In his book *Coping with Family Violence* Morton

Child abuse can take many different forms. This young victim entered an emergency shelter with burns on his arm, cheeks, and head.

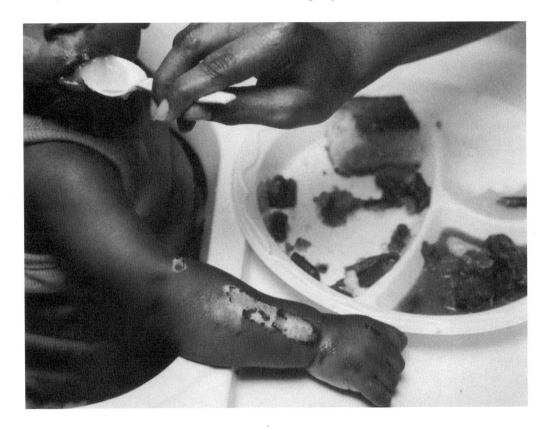

L. Kurland, M.D., points out that professional assistance can be found in most communities:

> There is a growing availability of experts in the field of family violence and sexual abuse. Many larger communities and counties have child guidance centers and family counseling centers that are becoming more and more experienced in the areas of family violence, marital discord, sexual abuse, and child abuse. . . .
>
> All of these professionals have dedicated their lives to understanding human behavior, to dealing with people's frailties, and to guiding others toward building their lives in positive directions, rather than negative ones.

The trauma of being physically or sexually abused as a child can affect an individual for the rest of his or her life. Such abuse can severely damage a victim's self-esteem. Because many children are taught at an early age that parents and other grown-ups know what is best for them, abused young people may come to feel that they deserved whatever mistreatment they received. In addition, victims often experience feelings of guilt, repressed anger, fear, and depression as a result of their abuse.

Abused children often suffer from guilt, anger, and depression. These feelings can remain with the victim for life.

Such negative emotions can often lead to problems for victims when they become adults. According to the November 2, 1992, issue of *Children Today*, the trauma of child abuse can often have long-term effects:

> The effects of child abuse are sometimes obvious even decades later. The effects are often pervasive: mental, physical, *and* social in nature. Suicide, violence, delinquency, drug and alcohol abuse and other forms of criminality are frequently child-abuse related.

A growing national crisis

The frequency of child abuse crimes committed in our nation has surprised and shocked many people. According to the U.S. Advisory Board on Child Abuse and Neglect, 2.4 million reports of suspected child abuse were filed in the United States in 1989. The *Los Angeles Times* published the results of a national phone survey in 1985. The results of the survey revealed that 22 percent of the women and 16 percent of the men surveyed had been sexually abused before the age of eighteen.

In 1986 the National Committee for Prevention of Child Abuse estimated that one million children are sexually abused each year. Of those, 71 percent are girls. Physical and sexual mistreatment of children has caused public outrage. Many child care experts have become outspoken in their criticism of the nation's failure to effectively protect children from such harm. These experts believe that child abuse threatens the nation's moral integrity and contributes to the destruction of the society. In 1990 the U.S. Advisory Board on Child Abuse and Neglect issued the following statement:

> Protection of children from harm is not just an ethical duty; it is a matter of national survival.
>
> It is bad enough—simply immoral—that the nation permits assaults on the integrity of children as persons. To make matters worse, such negligence also threatens the nation that shares a sense of community, that regards individuals as worthy of respect, that reveres family life, and that is competent in economic competition.

Victims of intimacy

Reports of violence against young people show that most child abuse is committed by parents, relatives, and friends rather than by strangers. Studies of case histories have shown this to be particularly true in cases involving sexual abuse. An article on child abuse appearing in a 1992 issue of *Children Today* states:

> Most offenders are known to the child; they are not strangers. They are fathers, uncles, brothers, grandfathers, aunts, stepfathers, neighbors, family friends or baby sitters. Child sexual assault happens most frequently in the victim's home or in the offender's home.

Most of those who mistreat young people had also been abused as children. This is known as the cycle of abuse, in which the victim of abuse becomes the abuser. Elda Unger, president of Free Arts for Abused Children, an organization that works with abused children, explains:

> In dealing with many parents and other relatives guilty of child abuse, we have found that the abusers at one time suffered from similar violence or abuse as children. This caused many of them as victims to repress anger, shame or fear which was later released in abusive behavior as adults.

A PICTURE OF A CHILD MOLESTER

Public concern for the protection of child abuse victims has led to the passage of laws in many states requiring citizens to report any suspected cases of abuse. In response to these reports social service workers are assigned to investigate the homes and families where abuse is reported. Because abuse investigations require detailed questioning of family members, and sometimes friends and even acquaintances, these investigations are nearly always deeply stressful for those involved. The intrusion into one's home by outsiders inquiring about suspected abuse is a humiliating experience. Yet there is no other way to determine if abuse is occurring. In *Recognizing Child Abuse: A Guide for the Concerned*, Douglas J. Besharov describes the difficult steps that must be undertaken in any abuse investigation:

> The determination that a report is unfounded can be made only after an unavoidably traumatic investigation, that is, inherently, a breach of parental and family privacy. To determine whether a particular child is in danger, caseworkers must inquire into the most intimate personal and family matters. Often it is necessary to question friends, relatives, and neighbors, as well as schoolteachers, day care personnel, physicians, clergymen, and others who know the family.

Protective custody

Social workers can proceed in several ways if they believe a young person is being abused. They can seek the help of a physician. Physicians have legal authority to hospitalize young people who may have been abused. They can be hospitalized for up to seventy-two hours to allow time for a physical examination and investigation. If investigating authorities conclude that the young person is endangered, state social service agencies have authority to take him or her into protective custody.

The removal of a young person from the family is a protective measure that has generated a high degree of controversy. In many instances social workers must decide whether it is best to place children in a foster home or to keep the family together and attempt to resolve the crisis as a unit. Social service workers are often reluctant to recommend that a child be placed in protective custody. Many feel that preserving the family unit is an invaluable aspect of child abuse prevention and treatment. Some experts believe that a child should be separated from his or her parents only as an extreme measure when caseworkers are convinced that the victim is in danger of suffering further abuse.

Social service workers must investigate reports of suspected child abuse. These investigations are often stressful for all involved.

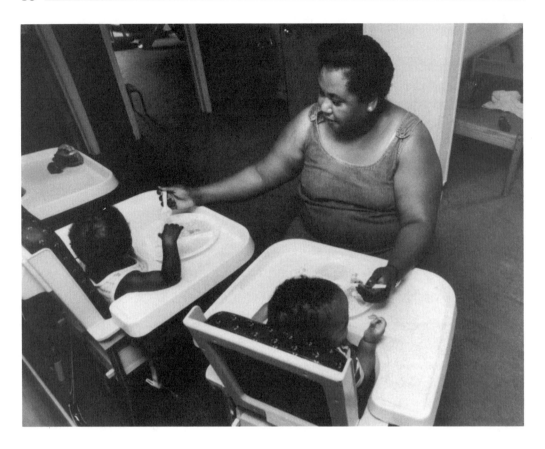

Two toddlers are fed at a shelter that provides refuge for abused children. Experts are divided on the wisdom of splitting up families by removing children from abusive homes.

Many social workers also feel that children placed in foster homes are at times as vulnerable to abuse as in their own homes. While many foster parents have provided safe homes for abuse victims, social workers have also reported cases of mistreatment in foster homes. In their book *Intimate Violence,* authors Richard J. Gelles and Murray A. Straus relate an example of how an outburst of abusive violence resulted in tragedy:

> An investigation revealed that a one-year-old child was being neglected by his mother. The mother was a teenage, single parent, who seemed both uninterested and unable to care for the needs of her son. The Department of Social Services chose to remove the young boy from his mother and to place him in a foster home. Within six months the boy was dead, beaten to death by his foster father.

Such tragedies indicate that placing children in foster homes does not assure their immunity from abuse. In addition, the trauma that a child can suffer from being separated from his or her family can often lead to severe emotional distress or psychological disorders in a child, according to Gelles and Straus:

> The protection offered victims is balanced against the disruption and potential destruction of their families. Children may also suffer from the treatment more than the abuse itself. The psychologist James Kent and his colleagues found that children removed from their natural homes and placed in a series of foster homes suffered long-term psychological problems.

A difficult choice

Researchers have concluded that despite the risk of further mistreatment, many abused children who were not removed from their homes often appeared to be more emotionally secure than victims who were separated from their families. Some experts attribute this to the belief that children who are placed in foster homes often feel that separation from their families is their fault or that they have been rejected by their parents. Feelings of guilt may result in intense emotional distress and damage to self-esteem.

In *Intimate Violence* Gelles and Straus report the following conclusion from their research: "Ironically, physically abused children who remained with their parents continued to be at risk for abuse, but did not evidence the same psychological deficits exhibited by the children placed in a series of foster homes."

In their book Gelles and Straus also cite one social worker's explanation of why many children placed in the protective custody of foster homes still continue to suffer:

I think you have to understand the typical pattern of abuse and neglect. Many children are told that the reason they are being hit or beaten is that they [the children] have done something wrong. If they are punished in other nonphysical ways—say they are locked in a closet—they are also told that they have been bad. From the children's point of view they suffer because they are bad. Moreover, they really have no way of knowing that what they are going through is different from what other children experience. When we remove an abused child to protect the child, the child may see this as the ultimate punishment for bad behavior. From the child's point of view the explanation for being removed may be, "I must have done something really wrong this time for my parents to give me up or send me away."

A young boy says goodnight to his foster mother. Abused children placed in foster homes may feel rejected by their parents and blame themselves for the separation.

These conflicts contribute to making child abuse one of the nation's most complex and difficult challenges. Many people differ in their opinions of what are the most effective and wisest methods to stop abuse. Such disagreements cause conflict and controversy and make society's attempts to eliminate child abuse a difficult and often frustrating process.

In spite of these difficulties, child care experts, educators, legal and medical experts, and others continue efforts to promote effective healing processes for child abuse victims and to protect all children from further mistreatment. Regardless of the great debates arising from the crisis of the mistreatment of young people, people committed to the protection of all children agree on one point: The challenge to end child abuse must be met if society is to effectively insure the welfare of each generation.

2

What Causes Child Abuse?

IN THE INTRODUCTION of his book *Coping with Family Violence*, Morton L. Kurland writes: "Violence, like charity, often begins at home. The roots and causes of violence in people's lives frequently lie in their earliest experiences." Investigations of the growing number of child abuse cases reported each year in the nation indicate that most child abuse originates within the young person's family.

In many cases the home in which the abuse occurred appeared to be that of an outwardly normal and happy family. Very often the internal conflicts of the family go unnoticed by outsiders. Sometimes, however, a teacher or other person observes evidence of physical mistreatment or emotional distress and reports these suspicions to a child-protection agency. In cases where such allegations, or accusations, of abusive behavior have been confirmed, caseworkers attempt to safeguard the child's welfare and to determine the reasons and causes of the abuse.

Research and analysis of the causes into why adults mistreat or neglect children is considered to be a critical aspect of society's efforts to prevent further child abuse. By gaining a greater

(Opposite page) A four-year-old girl, beaten by her father and suffering from malnutrition, peers out from her hospital crib. Understanding the reasons for abuse may help efforts to prevent it.

understanding of the factors that cause child abuse, experts hope to work more efficiently toward its prevention. Organizations such as the National Center on Child Abuse and Neglect, crisis intervention centers, and other agencies have concluded that some of the primary causes of child abuse can be attributed to substance abuse, poverty, and a family history of abuse.

Substance abuse

Many child care experts consider abuse of drugs and alcohol by adults to be one of the primary factors leading to child abuse. In 1992 the Department of Health and Human Services issued the following statement:

> The link between substance abuse and child abuse has strengthened over the years. Parental abuse of alcohol and use of other drugs has been identified as a major factor contributing to child maltreatment [mistreatment] and death. It is estimated that nearly 10 million children under age 18 are affected in some way by the substance abuse of their parents.

Substance abuse can lead to the physical, emotional, or sexual abuse of children. Adults' alcoholism and drug abuse may result in impaired

Alcohol and drug abuse often lead to depression, fits of violent rage, and impaired judgment, all of which can increase the risk of child abuse.

judgment, depression, or irrational outbursts of temper and fits of verbal or physical violence toward children. In addition, adults addicted to alcohol or drugs often neglect their children, failing to provide them with adequate food, shelter, clothing, and other material necessities.

Many cases of child abuse caused by drug or alcohol abuse often have tragic consequences. In Gary, Indiana, a woman taking cocaine left her nine-year-old daughter locked alone in an unheated apartment for nearly a week in January, when temperatures often reach freezing. As a result, both of the girl's legs were severely frost-bitten and had to be amputated.

Research has shown that substance abuse can have many devastating effects on families. One of the most damaging results of drug and alcohol abuse is family violence. A report compiled by a child-help center and published in the book *Wednesday's Children,* by Suzanne Somers, concludes:

> Alcohol is almost always involved in family violence. Up to 80% of all cases involve drinking, whether before, during or after the critical incident. . . . One out of every thirteen children with a substance-abusing parent is seriously abused each year.

So strong are the ties between substance abuse and child abuse that the Department of Health and Human Services has developed a wide range of programs addressing these problems together. These include research programs in the Administration for Children and Families, the Centers for Disease Control and Prevention, and the Office of Substance Abuse Prevention.

Poverty

In their efforts to understand the causes of child abuse, researchers have also explored the

Although child abuse occurs in families from all economic backgrounds, the extreme stresses of poverty may result in a high incidence of abuse.

relationship between poverty and abuse. Studies have shown a high incidence of child abuse in poor families. In 1985, 48.3 percent of abused children lived in families receiving welfare assistance in the program known as Aid to Families with Dependent Children (AFDC).

Such findings do not mean that abusive behavior occurs in all poor families or only in poor families. Studies clearly show that child abuse occurs in families from all economic levels and from every variety of racial, ethnic, and cultural backgrounds. Some researchers believe, however, that the extreme stresses resulting from a parent's inability to provide for his or her family may lead to child abuse. Parents who are unemployed and unable to find work may become depressed and angry. Their anxiety and frustration over being unable to earn a living and support their families can lead to outbursts of temper and even physical violence.

These findings are supported by a Department of Health and Human Services conclusion that "although child abuse occurs in all racial, ethnic, cultural and socioeconomic groups, physical abuse and neglect are more likely among people in poverty."

There is also a high number of teenage parents who live in poverty or are unprepared for the challenges of parenting. These parents are often too immature to deal with their children's needs, and this inability can lead to child abuse. One example of child abuse by a teenage parent appears in Kurland's book *Coping with Family*

A seventeen-year-old mother struggles with the challenges of raising her child in a poor, high-crime neighborhood in Brooklyn, New York. Teenage parents are not always equipped to deal with the challenges of parenting.

Some parents lack information about normal child behavior. They may punish and abuse a baby for crying, although crying is natural behavior for a baby.

Violence. Kurland relates the case of Ann B. who became pregnant at the age of sixteen and married her boyfriend.

The stress of becoming a mother and wife at a young age combined with the struggle to support her new family led to an unhappy home life for Ann. "I was scared all the time," Ann later said. "I didn't know what was going to happen or how I was going to take care of this new baby."

This fear and unhappiness eventually led Ann to outbursts of temper. Because she lacked the parenting skills to properly care for her child, she resorted to constant spankings to prevent him from crying. When a family doctor saw the welts and bruises on the baby, he suspected child abuse. An investigation led to the child's being placed in a foster home and Ann's entering a counseling program for abusive mothers.

Such cases reveal that parents living in poverty may be uninformed about normal infant and child behavior and unaware of how to provide proper care. They may not understand that an infant's crying is natural and that physically punishing the baby to stop the crying is harmful and abusive.

Joan I. Vondra, author of *Children at Risk*, believes that a direct relationship exists between poverty and the great number of child abuse cases reported among low-income families:

> That the majority of chronically [constantly] mal-treating families fall within the lowest social echelons [levels] is no coincidence. Economic, sociocultural, and interpersonal factors act jointly in the families to create a situation of severe economic stress, hardship, and dependency that has been cited as the single greatest threat in adequate family functioning.

A legacy of abuse

Research has shown that many adults who physically, emotionally, or sexually abuse children were themselves abused as children. The trauma of this mistreatment often results in severe emotional or psychological problems in adulthood. Adults who were victims of child abuse may carry intense feelings of repressed anger toward their abusers which they vent on their own children through cruel or violent behavior.

Some experts believe that this cycle of abuse is caused by the adult's need to justify the brutal behavior of his or her own parents. In their book *Straight Talk About Child Abuse*, Susan Mufson and Rachel Kranz state that many adults who abuse their children do so because they are unwilling or unable to admit that their own upbringing was abusive and wrong:

> For many parents who were abused as children, their reason for abusing their own children is that they need to prove that their parents were right. They do this by treating their children exactly as their parents treated them. . . . Many children find it easier to pretend that they are somehow responsible for the abuse, or that their parents are acting out of love, rather than to hold their parents responsible for acting badly. When those children grow up, they still don't want to admit their parents acted

badly. So they act just like their parents, because they reason to themselves their parents were acting out of love.

Experts also suggest that some adults who were abused as children imitate their parents' behavior out of a misplaced sense of duty to carry on the child-rearing practices from their own painful childhood. According to Mufson and Kranz, such parents were taught as children that they deserved such abuse, and they may communicate a similar message to their own children. Mufson and Kranz write: "Sometimes these parents decide that their children 'deserve' to be abused like they 'deserved' it when *they* were kids. Sometimes these parents identify with their own parents: 'He got to beat me, so now I get to beat you—it's my turn now.'"

Patterns are hard to break

In some cases an abuser simply does not know that there are other ways of relating to a child. That abuser might never have seen healthy interaction between a parent and child. In *Straight Talk* Mufson and Kranz explain: "Some people . . . are simply unaware of any other way of acting. They may believe that it's normal to beat a child or to vent one's anger with harsh insults. They may believe that it's normal to engage in sexually abusive behavior since that's the way they grew up."

Some abusers have witnessed how people in other families relate to each other. But patterns set in early childhood are hard to break. An adult who was abused as a child often repeats the only behavior he or she has experienced. In her book *Toxic Parents*, Dr. Susan Forward discusses the cycle of abuse:

> Physical abusers themselves often come from families to which abuse was the norm. Much of their adult behavior is a direct repetition of what they

..ABUSE BEGETS ABUSE...

experienced and learned in their youth. Their role model was an abuser. Violence was the only tool they learned to use in dealing with problems and feelings—especially feelings of anger.

Experts continue to research why adults mistreat young people in the hope that increased understanding of the roots of abusive behavior will result in its prevention. Although experts do not yet know all of the factors causing child abuse, they have concluded that many abusive parents lack self-control and fail to see the damaging effects of their own behavior toward their children. Dr. Forward states that abusive behavior is often an automatic, unthinking reaction to stress:

> We can only speculate why, but physically abusive parents seem to share certain characteristics. First,

they have an appalling lack of self-control. Physically abusive parents will assault their children whenever they have strong negative feelings that they need to discharge [release]. These parents seem to have little, if any, awareness of the consequences of what they are doing to their children. It is almost an automatic reaction to stress. The impulse and the action are one and the same.

Many abusers never recognize their behavior as problematic and many do not see the recurring patterns within their own families. For those who do, the realization is often painful. In *Toxic Parents* one abusive parent reveals her horror at seeing herself repeating the abuses of her own childhood:

Many abusive parents fail to realize the harm that they are inflicting on their own children. Coming to this realization can be extremely painful.

> I'm so ashamed of myself. I've slapped him in the past, but this time I really went berserk. That kid makes me so damned angry. . . . You know, I always promised myself that if I had kids, I'd never raise a hand to them. . . . I know what that's like. It's horrible. But without realizing it, I'm turning into that crazy mother of mine. I remember one time she chased me around the kitchen with a butcher knife!

The high incidence of child abuse committed by individuals who were themselves mistreated as children has provoked numerous child care experts to stress the necessity of breaking the cycle of abuse. Many adults who are survivors of child abuse have become increasingly more vocal and active in their efforts to raise the public consciousness regarding the need for professional treatment and counseling of abuse victims.

Seeking solutions to a national crisis

The necessity of protecting young people from abuse and neglect has become a national concern. The challenge of understanding the causes of child abuse and how best to protect young people from abuse must be met. In *Children Today* magazine, Anne Cohn Donnelly, who served as executive director of the National Committee for Prevention of Child Abuse, reaffirmed the need for diligent public protection of children and adolescents:

> Child abuse and neglect is a complex phenomenon that encompasses such individual factors as a parent's lack of understanding of child development, and environmental factors like poverty. To be successful, child abuse prevention efforts must ultimately take into account the various causes— both personal and societal—that play a role in the evolution of this problem.

> The consensus in the field [of child abuse prevention] is clear: No single approach, no single program is sufficient to prevent abuse; all elements of a comprehensive approach ultimately need to be in place. Yet our prevention efforts must begin somewhere.

3

Silent Victims

FOR MANY YEARS in the United States young people were expected to remain respectfully silent in the presence of adults. This tradition was expressed in the often quoted aphorism "Children should be seen but not heard."

The menace of child abuse is one of the factors that has compelled society to reevaluate this attitude. The total dependence of children on their parents and other adults has made them vulnerable to possible neglect and severe mistreatment by the very people responsible for their welfare and protection. Adults guilty of physically, emotionally, or sexually abusing children often attempt to conceal their acts by trying to force their victims to remain silent about their mistreatment.

Keeping secrets

These adults resort to many methods of persuading and sometimes scaring children into keeping their abuse a secret. They may convince young abuse victims that severe punishment or abuse was undertaken for their own good or because they behaved so badly that no other response was possible. An abusive adult may even convince a young abuse victim that discussion with others will destroy the family or lead to some other terrible result.

(Opposite page) Victims of child abuse often live with the daily torment of keeping their pain inside, unable to speak of the abuse out of fear or guilt.

Young people who believe that abusive behavior is normal or necessary are not likely to seek help. Nor are they likely to discuss their problem if they fear for themselves or other family members. In *Straight Talk About Child Abuse*, authors Mufson and Kranz describe the trap many young abuse victims fall into:

> People in physically abusive relationships prefer to believe that abusing adults are acting out of love or an appropriate need to impose discipline. This belief may mask the pain of being abused—but it also means that the abused person feels guilty and self-blaming. This makes it difficult to ask for help or to act to end the abuse.

Guilt is a common theme in many abusive households. Mufson and Kranz explain that guilt may

> come from being directly told by a parent or authority figure that the abused person has done something bad. In the case of the physical or emotional abuse, the authority figure may have explained the abuse by saying that the child is stupid, worthless, inconsiderate, or has some other terrible fault. In the case of sexual abuse, the authority figure may have told the child that he or she "asked for it," or behaved in a seductive way.

Other family members often also remain silent. Along with the abuse victim, they may even create a convincing picture of a loving, happy household. This is the picture outsiders may see even as the young victim suffers silently and alone. As Dr. Susan Forward writes: "Many abusive families are able to present a very 'normal' facade to the rest of the world. This apparent respectability is in direct opposition to the family's reality. It forms the basis of a 'family myth.'" Dr. Forward cites the case history of Kate, a young woman who was abused by her father. Kate describes the contrast between the reality and myth of daily life in her home:

To force a child to remain silent about abuse, adults may use threats or try to convince the child that the abuse was deserved.

I was raised in an upper class suburb outside St. Louis. We had everything money could buy. From the outside we looked like this perfect family. But from the inside . . . my father would go into these crazy rages. They usually came after he had a fight with my mother. He would just turn on whichever of us was closest. He would take off his belt and start strapping me or my sister . . . across our legs . . . on our heads . . . anywhere he could hit us. When he'd start in, I'd always have this fear he wouldn't stop.

A happy, loving family spends time together at a neighborhood park. A family troubled by abuse may also look happy and loving to outsiders.

The silent denial of substance abuse

Many adult survivors of child abuse confess that they have remained silent about their abuse out of deep feelings of loyalty to their parents. Such loyalty is particularly common in cases involving substance abuse. According to Dr. Susan Forward families of alcoholics or drug abusers generally feel driven to deny the existence of a substance abuse problem:

> Denial takes on gargantuan proportions for everyone living in an alcoholic household. Alcoholism is like a dinosaur in the living room. To an outsider the dinosaur is impossible to ignore, but for those within the home, the hopelessness of evicting the beast forces them to pretend it isn't there. That's the only way they can coexist. Lies, excuses, and secrets are as common as air in these homes, creating tremendous emotional chaos for children.

> The emotional and psychological climate in alcoholic families is much the same as in families where parents abuse drugs, whether illegal or prescription.

Denial of abuse is particularly common in families of alcoholics or drug abusers, where the child is also compelled to keep the substance abuse a secret.

Children who feel compelled by their families to deny or conceal their parents' alcoholism or

drug addiction are also often intimidated into remaining silent about their parents' abusive behavior. In Suzanne Somers's book *Wednesday's Children*, actress Cindy Williams recalled how she concealed for many years the emotional abuse she suffered by living with an alcoholic father:

> I was left in my father's care. It was really a time of anxiety and helplessness. How was Daddy going to act? Were we going to go out in the truck when he was drinking? If we did, he'd lock the doors and go inside the bar, leaving me in the truck. He'd buy me candy bars to keep me occupied and (I'm sure in his mind) happy. I can remember sitting in that truck watching the beer sign flash on and off while I was waiting for him: *Schlitz, Schlitz, Schlitz.* He had to get home before my mother did, because she'd flip out if she knew he was taking me to the bar. He'd say, "Don't tell." It was always to be our secret.

The silent terror of sexual abuse

Victims of sexual abuse are perhaps the most easily intimidated into remaining silent about their mistreatment. In addition to the mental confusion or bewilderment often resulting from such trauma, young people who have been sexually molested often suffer from many forms of emotional anguish. In addition to feelings of guilt or remorse resulting from their trauma, the young person may be threatened with bodily harm or even death by the abuser. In cases of incest the young person may be deeply influenced to remain silent about the molestation out of a sense of family loyalty and out of fear of upsetting other family members. Dr. Susan Forward explains:

> Ninety percent of all incest victims never tell anyone what has happened, or what is happening, to them. They remain silent not only because they are afraid of getting hurt themselves, but to a great

extent because they are afraid of breaking up the family by getting a parent into trouble. Incest may be frightening, but the thought of being responsible for the destruction of the family is even worse.

In an article written for *Family Law Quarterly*, Meredith Sherman Fahn, a lawyer for a California law firm often involved in child abuse cases, voices a similar viewpoint:

> In virtually every case of . . . child sexual abuse, the only witnesses are the abuser and the child victim. And there is always a blanket [total] denial: the abusive parent practically never admits it, the child is often intimidated into silence, and other family members allow themselves to remain comfortably unaware. In general, incest is a family secret.

Growing public concern about the sexual abuse of children has encouraged many adults to break their silence and speak out regarding their own experiences of sexual molestation. In an article published in *Good Housekeeping* magazine in November 1993, an anonymous writer recalled how being sexually molested as a child, first by her father and then by a neighbor, led to many

KIDS WHO LIVE IN HELL

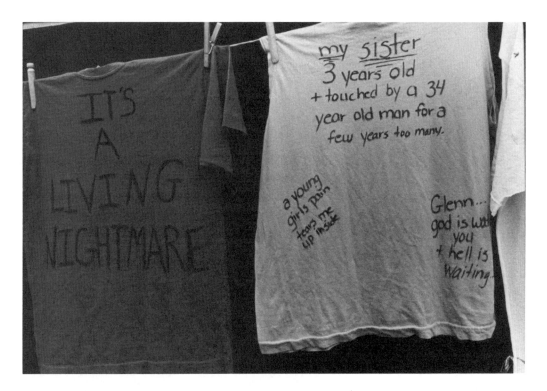

years of silent suffering: "I wasn't even sure what had happened, but somehow I knew I couldn't tell my parents. It would only confirm to my father how bad I was. And I sensed that my mother just wouldn't be able to cope with the news."

The writer further explained how this instinct proved correct. While receiving counseling as an adult, the victim decided to tell her mother about the sexual assault she had suffered from a neighbor as a child.

> A year into my healing, I called my mother and told her what had happened with the neighbor. For a while she just listened silently. But as her shock wore off, she told me my instincts had been right when I arrived home that first day my neighbor raped me. "I probably *couldn't* have handled it," she confessed. "Back then, sexual abuse just wasn't dealt with. I had no idea what the signs were and didn't even notice the changes in you. I'm sorry. I'm so sorry I wasn't there for you."

Adult survivors of child sexual abuse are becoming increasingly vocal about their experiences. One Massachusetts program encourages survivors to express their anger and other feelings through messages written on t-shirts. The t-shirts are hung for public display.

In addition to fear and bewilderment, young victims of sexual abuse often suffer deep feelings of shame and social isolation. Many victims feel intense guilt about having been molested. This guilt makes it difficult for them to believe they will still be accepted by their friends and other people. Such anxiety is especially traumatic for boys who have been molested by an adult male. According to some experts such victims often believe they will be abandoned by their friends or excluded from group or team activities. In

Molestation by an adult male can be particularly traumatic for boys, who often feel tremendous shame and may fear the stigma of being labeled a homosexual by their peers.

an article appearing in *People* magazine on February 7, 1994, David Finkelhor, an expert in child abuse, states:

> The shame issue makes it hard for adolescent boys to be in a group—especially given the stigma of homosexuality. . . .

> Feelings of guilt—"I must have brought this on"—must be addressed. The child must learn to trust adults again but also must learn to take control and deal with manipulative adults.

The increasing rate of suspected child abuse cases reported in the nation and the increasing number of abuse survivors voluntarily recounting personal experiences of their mistreatment indicate the severity of the problem. Many published accounts by victims vividly recount the horrors and personal devastation suffered from their abuse. Such accounts, along with the growing volume of research into child abuse, has had a great impact on public concern. The critical need to protect the silent victims of child abuse through enlightened awareness of their plight is reflected in a statement written by Dr. Timmen L. Cermak in the foreword to Suzanne Somers's book, *Wednesday's Children:*

> The universal human impulse is to deny abuse, whether you perpetrated it or suffered it. But the price of silence and denial is far too great. Each story tells us that emotional freedom depends upon breaking the bonds of silence. To gain this freedom, the victims of abuse must find the courage to speak truthfully about their experience. One of the primary sources of their courage is our willingness to listen. This is the most important contribution we can make to the safety needed to deal with the excruciating reality of their lives.

4

Child Abuse and the Media

A ROUTINE TRIP to the supermarket today can very likely serve to remind an individual of the great public concern over child abuse. Paper grocery bags and milk cartons featuring pictures of missing children, as well as shopping carts posted with signs displaying child abuse hot-line telephone numbers, have become common sights. These items are further evidence of the growing national awareness of the neccessity of protecting young people from mistreatment and violence.

Such widespread concern is in great part due to the public attention drawn toward the issue of child abuse by the mass media. In recent years the focus of much of this coverage by television, radio, magazines, and newpapers has been directed at the reporting of abuse cases involving charges of sexual molestation. The media have also produced numerous documentaries and public service programs on child abuse. In addition, the growing willingness of adult survivors of child abuse to emerge from anonymity and publicize their experiences has further alerted society to the severity of this problem.

The intense media coverage has provoked strong feelings in readers and viewers ranging

(Opposite page) Singer Michael Jackson, accused of sexual molestation, professes his innocence in a televised broadcast. Some people maintain that the media focus on the sensational aspects of child abuse cases, ignoring the complexity of the issues involved.

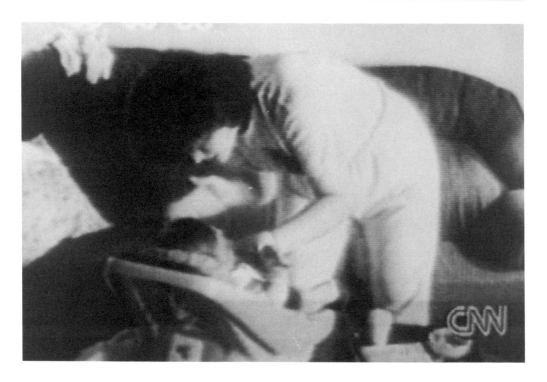

In this Cable News Network television image, a hidden camera captures a babysitter slapping a small child. Media coverage can both help and hinder the public's understanding of child abuse.

from compassion and concern to rage and hysteria. In-depth reporting combined with thoughtful presentation of facts and issues can increase public awareness and even inspire action. Simplistic reporting, on the other hand, meaning reporting that ignores the complex nature of the problems being covered, usually only adds to the myths and misconceptions about child abuse. The all too common focus on sensational events shows little regard for the depth and complexity of issues arising from child abuse.

Elda Unger of Free Arts for Abused Children sees media coverage as having both positive and negative consequences for society's understanding of child abuse. In an interview Unger said:

> I'd like to believe that we are very close to reaching the age of reason in recognizing child abuse as a major tragedy in society. The media has both helped and hindered in this process. There has been some wonderful informative reporting

done on child abuse that has greatly advanced public awareness of the problem. At the same time however, the sensational tabloid sort of abuse stories that persistently appear often distort or obscure the real issues that we need to address in order to begin the healing process and solve the problems.

Mass communication can greatly influence society's attitudes toward child abuse. A greater awareness of the positive and negative effects of media coverage on this issue can provide valuable insights into how many of those social perceptions are formed.

Heightened public awareness of child abuse

Public recognition of child abuse in general and child sexual abuse in particular represents a positive change from the days when people refused to acknowledge openly that such mistreatment occurred. Much of the news coverage of recent years has helped alert society to the plight of these children. In his book *Recognizing Child Abuse,* Douglas Besharov, former director of the National Center on Child Abuse and Neglect, writes:

> News stories daily remind us that children are brutally [mistreated] by their parents—the very persons who should be giving them love and protection.

The seven-year-old boy in the photograph, displayed by a police spokesman, was held as a virtual prisoner by his parents, who kept him locked in a bathroom for years. News coverage of such horrific abuse cases has helped to heighten public awareness of the problem.

Arnold Shapiro produced and co-wrote the documentary, "Scared Silent," which earned critical acclaim for its compelling exploration of the problem of child abuse.

Children are beaten until their bodies no longer heal, they are scalded with boiling water, they are starved and so dehydrated that their skin shrivels around their fragile bones, they are sexually assaulted and forced to perform all sorts of perverted acts, and they are locked in closets or tied to bed posts for days on end. Abused and neglected children are in urgent need of protection—protection that can be provided only if individual citizens are willing to help.

To a great extent media interest in child abuse has added to public concern. This concern has led to the development of many public service organizations and programs. Among the most prominent organizations in this field are the American Humane Association, the National Center on Child Abuse and Neglect, and the Child Assault Prevention Project. These and many other associations are dedicated to the prevention of child abuse and the protection and care of abused children.

Public service programs

The television medium has produced numerous documentaries and public service programs focusing on the subject of child mistreatment in the United States. One of the most important programs aired was the documentary "Scared Silent: Exposing and Ending Child Abuse," hosted by television talk show host, Oprah Winfrey.

Produced and cowritten by Arnold Shapiro, "Scared Silent" focused on prevention of sexual, emotional, and physical abuse. The program aired simultaneously in 1992 on the CBS, NBC, and Public Broadcasting Service (PBS) television networks. It was the first time in the history of television that a nonnews event was carried in prime time by three broadcast networks at the same time. A special National Child Abuse Hotline number was shown during the program urging viewers with abuse problems to call. As a

result of the program's broadcast, more than 112,000 calls were received by the hot line.

"Scared Silent" spotlighted six true stories of several generations of child abuse and profiled both the victims and their abusers in an effort to discover how abuse begins and how it can be stopped. The documentary won wide critical acclaim for its compelling perspective on child mistreatment. In the September 7, 1992, issue of *Newsweek,* writer Joshua Hammer praised Shapiro's production for its straightforward, if occasionally emotional, treatment of the causes and costs of abuse:

> "Scared Silent" does an admirable job of exploring the [troubled emotions and actions] of child abusers, exposing the horrific cost to its victims and explaining why it can remain a secret even to members of the immediate family.

> . . . The program lapses occasionally into the sappiness of a TV Movie of the Week: As Del and his daughter reunite, folk singers warble, "If we ever meet again, can we still be friends?" on the

In 1994 CBS aired "Break the Silence," a follow-up to "Scared Silent." In this animated scene from the documentary, which targeted children ages eight to fourteen, a physically abusive stepfather is depicted as an octopus with belts for arms.

A PBS documentary about the trial of day care center owner Robert F. Kelly Jr. (pictured) suggested that leading questions may have brought about an unjust child abuse conviction.

soundtrack. Still, "Scared Silent" deserves credit for humanizing both victims and victimizers. It offers no [quick] therapy sessions to restore dysfunctional families to health. But it holds out the hope of rehabilitation—and the inspirational example of a few tortured individuals willing to bring their darkest secrets to light.

Encouraged by the dramatic public response, the television medium has continued to produce other film studies focusing on the problem of child abuse. In the summer of 1993 PBS aired a documentary titled "Innocence Lost: The Verdict," produced by Ofra Bikel. The film offered a compelling look at the trial of Robert F. Kelly Jr., who in April 1992 was the first of seven people to be convicted of sexually abusing a dozen children in a day care center in Edenton, North Carolina. Kelly was a co-owner of the center. He is currently serving twelve consecutive life terms.

The film raised a question about Kelly's guilt. Kelly denied that he abused any of the children. The film suggested that improper investigating procedures may have led to Kelly's being unjustly imprisoned. The case against Kelly and his codefendants began in 1988 with a child's complaint about being slapped. This complaint led to an investigation resulting in a full-fledged sexual abuse case. Bikel's documentary suggests that the suspects were convicted based on information obtained from the children by leading, or suggestive, questions of interviewers and not supported by witnesses or evidence. Such productions reflect society's growing concern over the many and varied aspects of child abuse involving both perpetrators and victims.

Growing public involvement

Child abuse prevention has also become a major government concern. In 1990 the Department of Health and Human Services sponsored a special child abuse initiative that called for nationwide participation in preventing child abuse. The initiative encouraged greater cooperation between citizens, government, and community organizations to increase public awareness of child abuse. It urged all sectors of society to combat child abuse.

The campaign promoted the broadcast of video and audio news releases about child abuse prevention and treatment programs. In addition, Secretary of Health and Human Services Louis W. Sullivan and Marilyn Van Derbur Atler, a former Miss America and victim of childhood sexual abuse, taped public service announcements that were shown on television.

Such examples of positive media coverage indicate the tremendous potential of the media to constructively promote greater public awareness of child abuse issues and encourage affirmative action in society. Much of the publicity created by the media about child abuse, however, has produced negative results. One significant example of this is the sensational coverage by the media of highly publicized cases of suspected sexual abuse.

A landmark trial

One of the most widely publicized trials involving charges of suspected sexual molestation was the McMartin Pre-School case which commenced proceedings on July 13, 1987, at the superior court of Los Angeles. The trial followed three and a half years of investigations of allegations by McMartin students that they had been sexually molested and forced to participate in satanic rituals by the school's owners, Raymond Buckey and his mother Peggy McMartin Buckey.

Investigations of these allegations provoked widespread alarm among the parents of other children who attended the McMartin Pre-School. This

Raymond Buckey (center) and his mother Peggy McMartin Buckey plead innocent to charges that they sexually molested students at their day care center. The intense media coverage focused primarily on sensational accusations, including that they forced children to take part in satanic rituals.

concern soon grew into a general panic when the Manhattan Beach police issued two hundred letters to other parents of McMartin students inquiring about possible cases of sexual molestation involving Ray Buckey as the primary suspect.

The trial received heavy coverage by the media, which reported horrifying accounts of sexual molestation. In addition to these charges, media coverage of the trial involved lurid stories by children claiming they had been forced to dig up human corpses from a cemetery or jump out of airplanes.

The McMartin case became the longest and costliest criminal trial in U.S. history. The trial lasted for nearly three years. On January 18, 1990, the four-woman, eight-man jury brought in a verdict that acquitted the Buckeys of all but thirteen counts.

Many experts have criticized the media for their sensational coverage of the McMartin trial. Such coverage, they felt, presented a distorted view of the case to the public. In an article published in the *National Review* in February 1990, Douglas Besharov stated:

> Initial reports about McMartin highlighted disgusting tales of animal murder and bizarre behavior which, for months, were reported as true, not only by the tabloids, but our most respected news organizations. In 1984, for example, on ABC's newsmagazine *20/20*, reporter Tom Jarriel referred to the pre-school as "a sexual house of horrors."

Many critics believe that the media focused excessive attention on gruesome and shocking stories involving the case in order to capture the public's attention and gain high ratings. In Besharov's estimate, such sensationalistic coverage was unprofessional and showed little regard for the serious and complex nature of the accusations being made.

> It's easy to see why the media emphasized the most-sensational aspects of the case. As [an article in] *The New Republic* . . . explained, "A lot of the graphic horror stories in the press are little more than child porn, published or broadcast because editors and producers want to titillate. And when they're not being salacious [vulgar], the media [are] being mawkish [overly sentimental] which sells almost as well."

Sacrificing quality to attract an audience

High-profile cases involving alleged sexual abuse of children continue to draw sensational media coverage. Such coverage is especially intense when a celebrity or well-known public figure is involved. The problem with these stories is that they are often built around rumors, speculation, and instant analysis. Every new and more-sensational accusation is printed or broadcast simply because someone said it and because it involves someone famous. It is also not uncommon

Accusations of sexual molestation against Michael Jackson set off a worldwide media frenzy.

for the media to interview people who represent themselves as experts on the subject of abuse. These so-called experts are often asked to analyze the accusations and states of mind of both accuser and accused, although they have had no contact with either. Ratings or readership may rise with this type of coverage, but the public's understanding of the sad and complex issues surrounding the sexual abuse of young people suffers.

The Michael Jackson case

Such was the case in the summer of 1993 when singer Michael Jackson was accused by a thirteen-year-old boy of sexually molesting the youngster. Because of Jackson's tremendous popularity and fame as an entertainer, the accusations stimulated great public and media interest. The allegations led to a six-month investigation that received worldwide media coverage.

In a court document Jackson's accuser claimed that the entertainer befriended the boy. Jackson often invited the child to spend the night at his home, and according to the plaintiff, it was during one of these visits that the boy was molested. Jackson has maintained his innocence throughout the investigation.

In a live televised broadcast from Jackson's Neverland Valley Ranch in California, on December 22, 1993, the singer professed his innocence. During this broadcast Jackson disclosed that, as a result of the allegations, he had been intensely questioned by authorities. The singer expressed bitterness over the widely publicized allegations of suspected sexual molestation. During the broadcast the distressed singer made an emotional public appeal: "Don't treat me like a criminal, because I am innocent."

To date, Michael Jackson has not been formally charged with any crime. On January 25, 1994, attorneys for Jackson disclosed that a settlement had been reached in the boy's civil case against the singer. Although the attorney for Jackson's accuser did not retract the allegations, his client agreed to drop the charges in return for a settlement estimated at an amount between $15 million and $20 million. According to Jackson's attorney, Johnny Cochran Jr., the settlement was not an admission of guilt. "Michael Jackson is an innocent man," asserted Cochran in an article published by *People* magazine in February 1994. "The time has come for Michael Jackson . . . to get on with his life."

There can be little doubt that the subject of child abuse interests the public and, therefore, interests the media. This assures that the media will continue to cover this vital issue.

The broadcast and print media can draw national attention to the plight of an abused child. This publicity can dramatically increase public awareness of child abuse. The quality of that awareness, however, can be greatly influenced by whether media coverage of such cases results in accuracy or distortion of the facts reported. By recognizing the profound influences, both good and bad, that often result from media coverage, we may gain a deeper understanding of the challenges to be addressed as we endeavor to eliminate child abuse in our society.

5

In Their Own Words

THE TESTIMONY IN A COURT of law by young children about child abuse cases is an issue of great controversy. For many years children were not considered to be competent witnesses in such proceedings. They were thought to be too immature to provide reliable testimony. Because young children have limited language skills and very little experience in what is considered appropriate behavior in society, they were thought to make poor witnesses.

Young witnesses

The increasing number of child abuse cases tried in the nation's courts, however, has caused this viewpoint to change. Since many cases of child abuse have no other witnesses than the victim and the abuser, prosecutors must question the children involved despite the difficulties of interviewing them as witnesses.

The 1990 passage of the Victims of Child Abuse Act marked the change in attitude toward children's testifying in abuse cases. This act treats children as competent witnesses under federal law. It acknowledges the testimony of children as being an essential part of the evidence to

(Opposite page) A victim-witness assistant prepares a young girl to testify in a child abuse case. As children are increasingly being used as witnesses in such cases, the legal system must make efforts to insure that they are being questioned carefully and objectively.

57

be considered in determining the guilt or innocence of an abuse suspect.

There are no definite statistics on the number of children who have been witnesses in family court or criminal proceedings. In 1993 child psychology researchers Stephen J. Ceci and Eduardus de Bruyn estimated that possibly 100,000 children have testified in such cases. Ceci and de Bruyn state in an article in *Children Today:* "As a result of society's reaction to dramatic increases in reports of abuse and neglect, children increasingly are being admitted as witnesses in juvenile criminal proceedings."

The legal system is challenged to insure that justice is served by protecting children and punishing abusers. It must also take care that innocent people are not unfairly punished. To accomplish these goals, most experts agree, young witnesses must be questioned carefully and objectively. As with any witnesses, their testimony must be balanced with other evidence and testimony.

Many researchers believe that children can be excellent witnesses. They have shown over time that they accurately remember major events in their lives even if they confuse some of the lesser details. In *When the Victim Is a Child* Debra Whitcomb writes: "Even after a one-year delay, children do not make false reports of sexual abuse, although they may mistakenly report certain facts about the incident in question."

Suggestive questioning

The concern about child witnesses stems not from the fact of their being children but from the influence adult interviewers may have on them during questioning. Researchers believe that a child's recollection of events can be influenced by suggestive questions from adults. Something as simple as encouragement from an adult interviewer may prompt a child witness to tailor his or her answers to obtain approval. Many conclude that children are likely to alter their testimony to conform to what they believe adults wish them to say. Such compliance may result in a distortion of the truth, which may cause an innocent person to be unjustly convicted of abuse.

Leading questions

Researchers have attempted to devise effective means of questioning that would enable children to recall critical details of encounters with possibly

A therapist questions a young girl to determine if she has been sexually abused. Such interviewers must be careful to avoid suggestive questioning, which can influence a child's recollection of events.

abusive adults. In order to achieve this, interviewers often ask leading questions, that is, questions that will encourage young people to discuss very specific events and feelings. Some experts believe that such questions are suggestive in nature and may lead a young person to believe that certain events occurred even if they did not. Such influence on children was affirmed by Lenore Terr, a professor of psychology at the University of California, San Francisco. In a 1991 *Time* magazine interview, Terr said: "Kids can be fed ideas they quickly come to believe are true."

Testing memory

The concern over the possibility of manipulating children's memories through suggestive questioning has resulted in numerous experiments. Through these experiments researchers have tried to learn more about the influence an adult interviewer may have on a young witness. In a study conducted by Stephen Ceci, a psychologist at Cornell University, preschool children were told a story about a character named Sam Stone. The children were told that he was not a nice man and that he broke toys and stole things.

After giving the children this information, a man identified as Sam Stone visited the classroom. He did nothing more than wander around the classroom for a few minutes and then leave. The children were subjected to suggestive questioning about this visit for two minutes each week for the next three months. The questions were similar in structure to those asked in actual child abuse cases. For example, the children were asked such leading questions as, "Remember that day Sam Stone visited and broke the toy stove? Did he do it on purpose or was it an accident?"

The purpose of this experiment was to help experts determine whether suggestive questions could influence a child's testimony.

Following this questioning, a researcher interviewed the children about Sam Stone's actions. Nearly all of the children under the age of five described events that never occurred. For example they said that Stone spilled chocolate, ripped a book, or did other things suggested to them in the questioning. When further questioned, half of the children claimed they personally saw the events, while the others said they heard about Stone's actions from someone else.

The troubled legacy of the McMartin case

Such experiments have led experts to conclude that children can be influenced by adult interviewers and that the resulting testimony can badly hurt a person who is accused but possibly not guilty of committing abuse. This issue of manipulating testimony through leading questions and suggestive responses became an important obstacle in the McMartin trial. The interviews of the children at the Children's Institute International were primarily conducted by staff member Kee McFarlane, who holds a master's degree in social work and had worked in abuse treatment programs for more than ten years. Despite her professional background, McFarlane had almost no professional experience in obtaining evidence for trial.

Relying on her counseling skills, McFarlane employed the use of hand puppets and anatomically correct cloth dolls in her interviews with the children as a means of dramatizing their thoughts and recollections. During these sessions McFarlane would occasionally praise children who claimed they had been molested and reproach those who denied mistreatment. Defense attorneys later asserted that these methods appeared to encourage children to make accusations of abuse. McFarlane's methods raised doubt about the accuracy of accounts given by those children. These doubts were a factor in the case's outcome, which resulted in acquittal of Raymond Buckey and his mother on all but thirteen counts of child molestation.

Responding to a problem

The McMartin case provides a clear example of the problems that can occur when trying to obtain testimony from young people. Interviewers must carefully choose their words so as not to influence the child's answers. In a 1990 *National Review* article Douglas J. Besharov stated: "As the McMartin case demonstrates, for young children, the basic issue is whether an interviewer has used leading or suggestive techniques to implant a distorted or untrue version of such abuse in the child's mind."

Since the McMartin case, changes have been made in investigation procedures of child abuse cases. Many of the interview tactics employed during that trial, such as the use of anatomically correct dolls and strong suggestive questioning of child witnesses, are no longer used. In addition, interviews with young people called as witnesses are taped in order to answer possible later claims that children may have been manipulated by adults in their testimony. An article published in the January 29, 1990, issue of *U.S. New & World Report* offers a summary of the changes:

> Today, six years after the McMartin tale broke, sex-abuse cases are treated far differently in most places. Instead of being referred to regular police detectives, most charges go to investigators schooled in how to put sensitive questions to toddlers. Interviews are taped from the outset "so we can counter claims that the child was coerced or

coached," says Nancy O'Malley, a child abuse prosecutor in Oakland. No longer do probers immediately hand anatomically correct dolls to suspected victims, a technique now condemned as too suggestive. Cases are expedited [sped up] to avoid the problem of fading memories.

The McMartin trial was the most widely publicized child abuse case in national history. Press coverage focused sharply on the defendants and their young accusers and parents. Most child abuse cases, however, seldom expose child witnesses to such intense public scrutiny. Painstaking efforts are made to minimize the trauma of such proceedings.

A constitutional controversy

Legal experts are considering whether children should be spared the emotional distress of physically confronting their alleged abusers in court. Under the U.S. Constitution a person accused of a

A counselor uses anatomically correct dolls to question a sexually abused young girl. Since the McMartin case, such dolls are no longer used during interrogation of child witnesses.

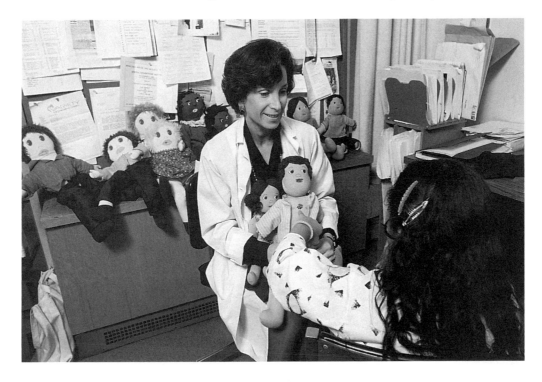

crime has a right to face accusers during trial proceedings. This right is guaranteed by what is known as the Confrontation Clause. This clause states: "In all criminal prosecutions, the accused shall enjoy the right . . . to be confronted with the witnesses against him."

An important legal ruling concerning use of the Confrontation Clause was made in October 1968 in the case of *Maryland v. Craig.* This case involved the trial of Sandra Ann Craig who was charged with the sexual abuse of a six-year-old child named Brooke Etze. Craig had been the owner and operator of a child care center that Brooke had attended.

Before the trial the judge ruled that Brooke and other child witnesses would suffer severe emotional distress and be unable to communicate if forced to confront Craig face-to-face. As a result of this finding the state of Maryland passed a law that allowed the children to testify on one-way, closed-circuit television.

The state's decision was protested by Craig on the grounds of the Confrontation Clause, claiming that the procedure denied the defendant a physical confrontation between herself and her accuser. Craig's objection was overruled on the grounds that the defendant had been given the right to observe and cross-examine the witness by way of closed-circuit television.

The Confrontation Clause has been the center of much controversy. Opinions of the clause vary within courts throughout the nation regarding the constitutionality of employing closed-circuit television as a medium for legal testimony. The decision in the case of *Maryland v. Craig* was upheld by the U.S. Supreme Court. The Supreme Court found that in this case the cross-examination of child witnesses by closed-circuit television satisfied the Confrontation Clause since it provided the accused with an opportunity to probe for and discover weakness in the witness's testimony. The use of closed-circuit television was held to be an essential means of accurately obtaining the testimony of these child witnesses.

Employing the use of closed-circuit television to obtain the testimony of young people is encouraged by researchers Eugene Arthur Moore, Pamela S. Howitt, and Thomas Grier. In *Juvenile and Family Court Journal,* these researchers wrote in 1991:

> The legal system must become sensitive to the special developmental characteristics of children and respond in a way which maximizes the likelihood that they will testify effectively. The *Craig* majority took an important step on the road to that goal.

Court schools

Another important step toward helping young people prepare for testimony is the court school. Court schools have been set up across the nation. Many are run by social service agencies or sponsored by children's advocacy centers.

Court schools are designed to help reduce the anxiety children often feel when testifying in court. The goals of court schools are to provide young people with information about going to court and to teach them the roles and responsibilities of people who work in court. Because children are often intimidated by adults, many court schools include programs that give children an opportunity to play the roles of judges, attorneys, and witnesses in simulated trials in order to improve their understanding of the trial process.

In an August 1993 article in *Children Today* Claire Ellis, who heads the Law Enforcement Child Abuse Project, summarized how court schools have benefited both adults and children involved in the program:

Witnesses appear before a judge during a typical day in court. Because testifying in court can be intimidating for children, court schools have been created to teach children about the trial process.

Court School has been enriching for all of us. We continue to work across disciplines exploring new ways of helping abused children. Children gain confidence and feel supported. Prosecutors gain the experience of working with children. Volunteers and law students gain a better understanding of the complexities of the judicial system. And the public is better served.

A continuing quest for truth

Efforts by legal and child care experts to provide effective and fair means of attaining justice for both adults accused of abuse and young people who have been abused continues to be a complex and often controversial process. In a March 1991 article in *Time* magazine writer Jerome Cramer concluded:

> What these researchers [members of the American Psychological Association] and others are finding out is that truth for a child can be blurred, especially in periods of stress, such as during a trial. To protect children from sex crimes and adults from unfounded accusations child welfare workers and prosecutors will have to take special care when searching for the truth.

In the *University of Cincinnati Law Review* Katherine A. Francis writes of the continuing challenges facing the criminal justice system regarding child abuse:

> Criminal prosecutions for the physical, emotional, or sexual abuse of children in which the child victims testify against the accused pose a difficult task for the courts. They must balance the constitutional rights guaranteed the accused with the physical and psychological well-being of the child victim/witness so that the courts may attain the societal goal of the criminal process: finding the truth.

CHILD RAPE HURTS FOR A LONG LONG TIME

6

Pathways to Healing

AS A SURVIVOR of child abuse, the late journalist Randy Shilts recalled in Suzanne Somers's book *Wednesday's Children* the intense emotional suffering he had endured early in life: "When I was nine years old, I resolved that I wouldn't cry no matter how hard my mom beat me. To this day I can't cry. It's horrible. Crying is an expression of feelings, and I stopped feeling."

Shilts's description of his reaction to his mistreatment as a child is a poignant, or moving, account of how the trauma of child abuse can continue to have disturbing effects on its victims throughout their lives. The emotional and psychological injuries inflicted on children from physical, sexual, or verbal abuse can often be devastating.

In her article published in the November 2, 1992, issue of *Children Today*, Anne Cohn Donnelly offered a forthright assessment of the tragic effects of child abuse on both individuals and society:

(Opposite page) Marchers protest child sexual abuse. As this poster asserts, victims of child abuse suffer the emotional pain of abuse for many, many years.

> Child abuse hurts. The aftereffects, which are well documented, are devastating. Abused children suffer a wide range of emotional, developmental and physical problems, both acute and chronic.

69

The trauma of abuse leads some young people to run away from home and turn to alcohol or drugs.

Some children die. These problems often precipitate such social ills as teenage runaways, adolescent prostitution, drug and alcohol abuse, academic failure and school truancy, and juvenile delinquency.

Child abuse is costly, both in terms of human suffering, and in terms of the financial costs that must be borne by society to remedy the social and psychological maladies emanating from child maltreatment.

The rising number of child abuse and child neglect cases reported in this country has become a national concern. In recent years this concern has led to the creation of numerous programs geared toward counseling victims in their recovery from the trauma of such mistreatment.

Child abuse prevention

Safeguarding young people from physical or sexual mistreatment has become a top priority among child care experts and social workers. By developing educational programs that will increase young people's awareness of the causes and dangers of child abuse, experts hope to aid in its prevention. Child abuse and neglect are complex problems that are influenced by many factors, including a parent's inability to understand the process of healthy child development and such environmental factors as poverty. In order to successfully prevent child abuse, society must evaluate and understand the various individual and social causes of child abuse. In her article in *Children Today*, Dr. Donnelly asserts: "The case for working to prevent child abuse before it occurs is clear. Prevention spares the hurt and can save lives and money."

In the summer of 1990, Secretary of Health and Human Services Louis W. Sullivan created an initiative calling for national participation in the prevention of child abuse and neglect. In this initiative Sullivan hoped to encourage greater active public involvement in community and government programs designed to combat child abuse.

The initiative promoted a child abuse prevention campaign called "Show You Care." The

A social worker calls on one of her cases in a public housing project. Social workers are among those searching for ways to prevent child abuse and neglect.

Secretary of Health and Human Services Louis W. Sullivan created an initiative calling for active public involvement in programs designed to prevent the mistreatment of children.

campaign included the organization of national and regional meetings to discuss local strategies for child abuse prevention and aiding the families of victims. "Show You Care" also called for cooperation between the Department of Health and Human Services and other federal agencies to improve services related to child abuse.

Federal sponsorship of programs directed toward child abuse prevention has encouraged increased participation at community, state, and national levels. Currently, all fifty states in the nation have enacted child abuse reporting laws, with specialized child-protection agencies established to investigate such reports.

Affirmative action against abuse

In order to promote healthy family lifestyles and reduce the risk of child abuse and neglect, the Family Intervention Center (FIC), the National Committee for Prevention of Child Abuse, and other groups conduct seminars, workshops, and other educational programs around the country. Such programs, experts believe, will help increase public awareness of abuse and aid in its prevention.

One program with this objective began in September 1990, when the FIC hired health educator Dayna Jornsay to work alongside teachers and administrators in the Sto-Rox school district in Pennsylvania. Jornsay collaborated with them in an effort to study critical health issues such as drug and alcohol abuse, teen pregnancy, and child abuse. Jornsay and the school district then devised a set of twenty-five prevention lessons aimed at teaching students how to ask for help if they are subjected to abuse and other skills designed to promote general health awareness.

Instead of creating special courses focusing on each health issue, the school district decided to revise the general health curriculum to include life skills and specific information about drugs, alcohol, and child abuse. The collaboration with the FIC also resulted in a community health fair designed to provide students with projects to teach some specific lesson about health or child abuse. Sponsored by the school board and several community agencies, the health fair was held in the school's gym and attended by more than four hundred students. Seventeen booths were constructed featuring displays and activities with various health themes.

One exhibit compared myths and facts about abuse. One of the myths cited in the display was the assumption that young people often lie or fabricate stories about abuse. This myth was countered by the statement that young people do not invent stories about their own sexual abuse.

During a press conference introducing legislation designed to crack down on child abuse, a doctor demonstrates how shaking can injure an infant. The federal government has shown a commitment to child abuse prevention through legislation and sponsorship of programs.

The display further defined incest as an adult behavior rather than a child's fantasy.

Encouraged by the students' enthusiastic response to this event, Sto-Rox school administrators and teachers organized a second health fair for 1991 that focused on how young people can get help and protection if abuse is occurring in their household. Such activities, according to Dayna Jornsay, are invaluable in raising youth awareness. Summarizing the health fair's objectives, she said:

> The kids learn how to ask for help. That's a primary skill for prevention of abuse. These types of activities give adolescents a chance to meet the faces behind the telephone numbers [of help lines and agencies] and to be more comfortable using the services available in their community.

Crisis intervention centers

Among the services available in most communities are crisis intervention centers. These centers offer emergency counseling and assistance, usually by telephone and sometimes in person. A crisis center can offer a place for a parent to turn at moments of extreme stress, frustration, and rage—when the risk of abuse is greatest. Crisis intervention centers can provide a safe and supportive environment in which parents receive immediate counseling during critical times of emotional distress. Angry or stressed parents sometimes bring their children to these centers out of fear that they will physically abuse their children. By providing temporary care for these children, crisis intervention centers can assist the parents in calming themselves and receiving counseling.

In April 1982 New York City's Foundling Hospital opened the Crisis Nursery to offer parents such resources as child care, health care, and other social services. Vincent J. Fontana, a medical director and chief pediatrician at Foundling Hospital, and Valerie Moolman, an author, explain the principles of the Crisis Nursery program in their book *Save the Family, Save the Child:*

> "Crisis Nursery" sounds like a contradiction in terms. It isn't. Nor is it an intensive care unit for babies. The Crisis Nursery at New York City's Foundling Hospital is an emergency refuge for children at risk of being damaged by their parents—parents desperately in need of relief from stress. The children brought to the Crisis Nursery seldom need much medical care. What they do need is a respite from their troubled parents, just as their parents need a respite from them.

Crisis intervention centers offer counseling and support to parents during times of great stress, when they are most likely to take their frustration and anger out on their children.

The authors explain that a twenty-four-hour-a-day, seven-days-a-week help line was made available to distressed parents who feared that a domestic crisis could lead to child abuse. The public awareness program featured posters displaying the center's phone number and inviting overburdened people to bring their children to the center for assistance.

Fontana and Moolman believe that such programs are effective in helping to break the cycle of abuse. In their book they explain how they hope such intervention as aid to parents can act as a healing process:

> Our hope is that if the parent leaves the . . . child with us for two or three days and nights, it will not only give the child a break but allow the parents a cooling-off period without having that child around to pick on. At the same time we initiate crisis intervention and longer-term treatment for striking-out parents with the purpose of ending, once and for all, the cycle of abuse that persists from generation to generation.

Art heals

Halting abuse is an ultimate goal of society, and prevention and intervention programs have made significant progress in achieving that goal. Despite such efforts, however, child abuse still occurs. Abuse victims have special needs that require special attention and care. Free Arts for Abused Children in Los Angeles is one such program. FAAC introduces creative arts activities to victims of child abuse as outlets through which they can increase their self-esteem, express their emotions, and gain self-confidence.

Free Arts for Abused Children currently includes about 750 volunteers and is affiliated with eighty residential-care facilities throughout California. The program actively recruits and trains volunteers, who are then placed in one of

At Free Arts for Abused Children, young victims of child abuse are encouraged to express themselves through art. Art provides an outlet for communication and for boosting self-esteem.

these eighty facilities to work with abused children. The FAAC volunteers work with children and adolescents in projects involving dance, drama, writing, music, painting, sculpting, and film.

These projects are aimed at encouraging children's own sense of self-worth and building character by encouraging them to channel emotions, release anger, and use their imaginations. Elda Unger, president of FAAC, summarized the organization's philosophy of creative nourishment of abused children:

> We have a motto at Free Arts that expresses the essence of what we endeavor to achieve in service.

The motto is: "Art Heals." The whole idea is to encourage the creative process in children through artistic expression that will help them to communicate better and to have greater self-esteem.

The Children's Court House

One of the most successful FAAC programs involves the organization's affiliation with the Edelman Children's Court House in Monterey Park, California. Child abuse trials are held in this courthouse.

The Children's Court House was created as a model for trials of child abuse cases. Before the courthouse's construction, child abuse cases had always been tried in regular courtrooms. All of the twenty-five courtrooms in the Children's Court House were designed to provide a comfortable and secure environment for the children and include such facilities as smaller seats and tables. Judges at this facility sit on lower benches than they would occupy in a traditional courthouse. Mediators work with parents and children in an effort to find solutions that will be good for all involved. In addition, a section of the courthouse has been designed and furnished to provide a friendly and nonthreatening waiting area for young people.

In an interview, Elda Unger explained FAAC's involvement with the Children's Court House:

The Children's Court House is extremely "child-friendly." Our volunteers work with children in this environment on the various art projects as they wait for their cases to be tried. Very often the parents of these children become involved in the projects and have discovered the joy of creative interaction with their children they had never known before. The workshop program in the courthouse has proven remarkably effective in relieving children of much of the stress involved in legal proceedings, and helping them to relax in a creative and active fun-filled environment.

The creative arts programs of FAAC also include activities geared toward promoting the healing of the parents of abused children. Volunteers work with parents of abused children on various art projects, such as paintings and col-

Edelman Children's Court House strives for a non-threatening, child-friendly environment. This mural at the courthouse features self-portraits of some of the many abused children who have come to the courthouse to testify.

oring projects, for eight weeks. Many of the parents who take part in the FAAC program also undergo professional counseling in an effort to change their behavior.

Opening up communication

Therapists from treatment programs are often invited to sit in with volunteers and watch the art activities. Art projects provide a form of therapy that opens up different means of communication between parents and their children. The creative arts projects vary from week to week and include activities in writing, sculpting, and painting. Parents and children are encouraged to work together on some projects. According to Elda Unger the program has greatly improved the relationships between many parents and their children:

> Such activities have often led to the beginnings of a wonderful rapport between parents in counseling and their children. Kids will say after such sessions: "I never realized that my mom or dad could ever be this fun!" So it's a wonderful opportunity for parents and children who have had a troubled history of abuse to rediscover each other in a professionally guided and creative environment.

All FAAC volunteers are specially trained for working with abusive adults and abused young people. Volunteers do not counsel their clients; counseling is left to professionally trained therapists and psychologists. But volunteers are important because they provide parents and children with opportunities to creatively interact with each other and encourage greater communication. "The primary aim of Free Arts is to create a safe and nurturing environment to encourage artistic expression and rekindle imagination in children through the arts," Unger said.

The involvement of children in artistic activity may do more than promote healing. Children's

Volunteers at Free Arts for Abused Children encourage interaction and greater communication between children and parents.

creative expression can also provide poignant statements that alert people to the plight of these children. The following verses were composed by a thirteen-year-old girl involved in the FAAC writing program and is an eloquent commentary on the tragedy of child abuse:

Where Is Sadness?

sadness is
    not having parents
    when you need them
sadness is
    not having friends
sadness is
    not having pets
    when you need them very much
sadness is
    not having girlfriends
    and boyfriends
sadness is
    not being in a home
    when you really need one
that hurts.

Organizations
to Contact

The following organizations provide services and information relating to all aspects of child abuse.

American Academy of Child and Adolescent Psychiatry (AACAP)
3615 Wisconsin Ave. NW
Washington, DC 20016
(202) 966-7300

The AACAP is an association of psychiatrists trained in child psychiatry. The association publishes *Facts for Families*, which includes information sheets including "Child Sexual Abuse" and "Child Abuse—the Hidden Bruises."

American Humane Association (AHA)
Children's Division
63 Inverness Dr. East
Englewood, CO 80112-5117
(303) 792-9900

The function of the children's division of the AHA is to protect children and assist in healthy family development by encouraging community programs of care for children and families. The association also publishes books, fact sheets, and a quarterly magazine, *Protecting Children*.

American Professional Society on the Abuse of Children (APSAC)
332 S. Michigan Ave., Suite 1600
Chicago, IL 60604-4537
(312) 554-0166

The APSAC works toward the improvement of services involving child abuse prevention, treatment, and research. The society publishes a quarterly newsletter, *The Advisor*, and the *Journal of Interpersonal Violence*.

National Assault Prevention Center (NAPC)
Child Assault Prevention Project (CAP)
PO Box 02005
Columbus, OH 43202
(614) 291-2540

The NAPC is dedicated to the prevention of violence through research and education. The center's Child Assault Prevention Project provides abuse-prevention services to children, teachers, and professionals. NAPC and CAP also publish brochures, videos, and books on child abuse.

End Violence Against the Next Generation, Inc. (EVANG)
977 Keeler Ave.
Berkeley, CA 94708-1498
(415) 527-0454

This is an organization dedicated to ending corporal, or bodily, punishment in schools. EVANG publishes a quarterly newsletter, and booklets including *The Influence of Corporal Punishment on Crime*.

Family Research Council (FRC)
700 13th St. NW, Suite 500
Washington, DC 20005
(202) 393-2100

FRC is a lobbying organization dedicated to reforming the child protection system. It has published the book *Free To Be Family* and the monthly newsletter *Washington Watch*.

For Kids Sake, Inc.
31676 Railroad Canyon Rd.
Canyon Lake, CA 92380
(714) 244-9001

For Kids Sake is an organization dedicated to child abuse prevention through education and intervention. Their facilities include a large research library on the subject of child abuse, as well as brochures on parenting and child safety. The organization also operates molestation-prevention programs.

Free Arts for Abused Children (FAAC)
11605 W. Pico Blvd., 2nd Floor
Los Angeles, CA 90064
(213) 479-1212

FAAC is a registered nonprofit organization dedicated to bringing the healing power of creative arts activities to young victims of child abuse who are residing in protective custody throughout Southern California. In addition, FAAC works with dysfunctional families through creative arts activities to enable these families to discover the mutually beneficial methods of communication.

National Committee for Prevention of Child Abuse (NCPCA)
332 S. Michigan Ave.
Chicago, IL 60604-4357
(312) 663-3520

The NCPCA is dedicated to the prevention of child abuse in all forms. The organization publishes and distributes a wide variety of material on child abuse and child abuse prevention.

Suggestions for Further Reading

Jim Haskins, *The Child Abuse Help Book*. New York: Addison-Wesley, 1982.

Robin Lenett with Bob Crane, *It's O.K. to Say No!* New York: TOR Books, 1985.

Angela Park, *Understanding Social Issues: Child Abuse*. New York: Aladdin Books, Gloucester Press, 1988.

Judith S. Sexias, *Living with a Parent Who Drinks Too Much*. New York: Greenwillow Books, 1979.

Susan Neiburg Terkel and Janice E. Rench, *Feeling Safe Feeling Strong*. Minneapolis, MN: Lerner Publications, 1984.

Works Consulted

Robert T. Ammerman and Michel Hersen, eds., *Children at Risk: An Evaluation of Factors Contributing to Child Abuse and Neglect*. New York: Plenum Press, 1990.

Douglas J. Besharov, *Recognizing Child Abuse: A Guide for the Concerned*. New York: Free Press, 1990.

Jerome Cramer, "Why Children Lie in Court," *Time*, March 4, 1991.

Anne Cohn Donnelly, "Healthy Families in America," *Children Today*, November 2, 1992.

Vincent J. Fontana and Valerie Moolman, *Save the Family, Save the Child: What We Can Do to Help Children at Risk*. New York: Mentor, 1991.

Susan Forward with Craig Buck, *Toxic Parents: Overcoming Their Hurtful Legacy and Reclaiming Your Life*. New York: Bantam Books, 1989.

Katherine A. Francis, "To Hide in Plain Sight: Child Abuse, Closed Circuit Television and the Confrontation Clause," *University of Cincinnati Law Review*, 1992.

Richard J. Gelles and Murray A. Straus, *Intimate Violence*. New York: Simon and Schuster, 1988.

Neil Gilbert et al., *Protecting Young Children from Sexual Abuse: Does Preschool Training Work?* Lexington, MA: Lexington Books, 1989.

Good Housekeeping, "Abuse Nearly Ruined My Life," November 1993.

Sylvia Hewlett, *When the Bough Breaks: The Cost of Neglecting Our Children*. New York: Basic Books, 1991.

Morton L. Kurland, *Coping with Family Violence.* New York: Rosen Publishing Group, 1990.

Eugene Arthur Moore, Pamela S. Howitt, and Thomas Grier, *Juvenile and Family Court Journal*, 1991.

Susan Mufson and Rachel Kranz, *Straight Talk About Child Abuse*. New York: Facts on File, 1991.

National Review, "Protecting the Innocent," February 1990.

People, "Dodging the Bullet," February 7, 1994.

Susan Schindehette et al., "After the Verdict, Solace for None," *People*, February 5, 1990.

Suzanne Somers, *Wednesday's Children: Adult Survivors of Abuse Speak Out*. New York: G. P. Putnam's Sons, 1992.

U.S. Catholic, "You Should Never Hit Kids," January 1992.

U.S. News & World Report, "The Child-Abuse Trial That Left a National Legacy," January 29, 1990.

Index

About the Author

Tom Ito is a freelance writer who resides in Los Angeles, California. His interest in the entertainment industry led him to publish *Yesteryears* magazine, a publication profiling television and radio celebrities, which he edited and distributed in the greater Los Angeles area from 1988 to 1990. Mr. Ito has served as a literary consultant for Hanna-Barbera Productions. He is listed in *Who's Who of Asian Americans* and is the author of *Conversation with Michael Landon*, a memoir written in tribute to the late actor.

Picture Credits

Cover photo by © 1991 Lew Lause/Uniphoto Picture
  Agency

AP/Wide World Photos, 46, 48, 50, 64, 72

Arnold Shapiro Productions, 49

Nick Arroyo/Atlanta Constitution, 9, 56

© Billy Barnes/Uniphoto Picture Agency, 75

© Jacques Chenet/Woodfin Camp & Associates, Inc., 63

Free Arts for Abused Children, 77, 79, 80

© Jeff Greenberg/Unicorn Stock Photos, 37

© Marilyn Humphries/Impact Visuals, 8, 41, 68

Evan Johnson/Jeroboam, Inc., 6

© Martin R. Jones/Unicorn Stock Photos, 38

© Andrew Lichtenstein/Impact Visuals, 20, 70

© D & I Mac Donald/Jeroboam, Inc., 13

© D & I Mac Donald/Unicorn Stock Photos, 36

© 1992 Ken Martin/Impact Visuals, 66

© Martha McBride/Unicorn Stock Photos, 28

Katherine McGlynn/Impact Visuals, 26, 27

James Motlow/Jeroboam, Inc., 32, 34

Reuters/Bettmann, 44, 54

Andy Sharp/Atlanta Constitution, 10, 12, 18

John Spink/Atlanta Constitution, 17, 71

© Ann States/SABA, 59

Uniphoto Picture Agency, 24

UPI/Bettmann, 22, 47, 52, 73

© 1993 Aneal Vohra/Unicorn Stock Photos, 42